AN AMISH QUILT FOR CHRISTMAS

BOOK 2 RACHEL

By

PAIGE MILLIKIN

Copyright © 2017

Paige Millikin

An Amish Quilt for Christmas

INTRODUCTION

Rachel has done something terrible.

Throwing the precious family heirloom on the fire seemed like a good idea at the time, but now Rachel has begun to regret her rash actions.

The anger and jealousy she feels continues to eat her up inside, and she finds that the only solace she can find is to throw herself into her art, away from her family.

But her questions don't stop and when she meets James, the kind hearted young man who begins to grow more important to her with every passing day, Rachel is forced to confront her past.

Will James still want to court her when he finds out what she did? And can she find the strength to tell her mother the truth, hoping that she will be able to forgive Rachel for what she's done?

Find out in this Amish Christmas story about family ties, forgiveness and love.

Paige Millikin

An Amish Quilt for Christmas

TABLE OF CONTENTS

Paige Millikin

LEGAL NOTES

Paige Millikin

CHAPTER ONE

Rachel Kollmorgen couldn't help but shoot a glance at her older sister as Emily left the house, saying something to their mother that Rachel couldn't hear. Their mother laughed and shooed her away, continuing to smile softly even after Emily had left the house.

Rachel gritted her teeth and turned away, trying to ignore the wave of guilt that sliced straight through her heart.

Paige Millikin

"Is everything all right, Rachel?"

"Everything's fine, mama," Rachel replied, blandly. "I'm just going to go to my room for a while." She picked up her pencils and paper and made to leave the room.

"Are you going to be drawing?"

Her mother's questions just delayed Rachel's exit, sending frustration shooting through her veins.

Turning back to her mother, Rachel tried to smile. "Yes, I was hoping to start a new piece and I have a couple more commissions to finish."

Her mother's warm smile did nothing but intensify Rachel's guilt.

"You are doing very well, Rachel," her mother continued, smiling. "Your father would be very proud of what you are doing to help support the family. I know I am."

An Amish Quilt for Christmas

"Thank you, mama." Now feeling more than a little nauseous, Rachel left the room and found the safety of her own bedroom.

Her room was her haven, the only place where she could be entirely alone. Her mother, sister, and brother knew to leave her be when she was inside, never interrupting her as she'd requested. Her art came to life here, in the solitude. She put everything she was thinking and feeling into each piece, although she never let anyone else know exactly what it was that drove her.

Putting another blank canvas on the easel in the corner, Rachel tried to ignore her swirling feelings. Her mother was always so kind and gentle, and she had no idea what Rachel had tried to do.

Even now, she felt sick over what she had done, although the anger remained.

A couple of months ago, Rachel had overheard her mother and Emily talking, only for Emily to exit from her mother's room with a bundle in her hands.

Paige Millikin

This had been the Christmas quilt, the one handed down for generations, and now it belonged to Emily.

The jealousy had hit Rachel squarely in the stomach.

Emily was the eldest and, since the quilt had been handed down from oldest daughter to the next oldest daughter, it was quite right that Emily should be the one to get it. But Rachel hadn't seen it that way. In her mind, it was just another way that Emily was outdoing her.

Not that it had ever been a competition, but since their father had died some years ago, Emily had been the one to shine. Rachel had overheard her mother talking about how much Emily had supported her, how she'd been able to shoulder the responsibility of bringing in some money to the family, while their mother tried to find her feet again without her husband by her side. And what had Rachel done?

Rachel had retreated into her shell, had chosen to hide herself away from the rest of her family. The loss of their father had been a shockingly painful blow and, instead of talking about what she felt and spending time with her family, Rachel had hidden herself away. Her art became the only thing she put her time and energy into, and, while the rest of the family banded together, Rachel had chosen her isolation.

Perhaps that was why she had done what she did.

Trying to start her sketch, Rachel noticed that her hands were trembling as her mind became filled with the memories of what she had done.

Her anger over what Emily had been given, her disappointment in herself over how distant she'd become from those who loved her, had made her do something impetuous. She'd taken the quilt that Emily had laid out on the line and had thrown it on a fire.

She hadn't even waited to watch it burn.

Paige Millikin

The moment she'd got back to the house, everything in her had screamed to go back and sort it out, to pull the quilt out of the flames and put it back where it belonged – but instead, she'd just gone to her room and shut herself inside. She kept trying to justify herself over and over, seeing the utter torment on Emily's face the day she'd come back without the quilt and, even when Emily had confronted her with the truth, Rachel had admitted it without even a word of apology.

Emily hadn't shouted at her or lost her temper. Instead, she'd just looked utterly devastated and confused. At the time, Rachel had enjoyed yelling at her sister all the things she'd kept inside for so long, but now those words turned to ash in her mouth. It wasn't Emily's fault that Rachel had hidden away from the family, or that her mother seemed to see Emily in a better light than Rachel. All of the choices Rachel had made had been her own.

Sighing to herself, Rachel tried to start again on her drawing, letting the pencil flow across the paper. The truth was, she didn't know how to get back to where she'd been before their father died. They'd been such a close family, always talking and laughing together, but now things were different. There was still laughter, still conversation, but Rachel had pulled herself back from that so much that she didn't know how to get back. She wanted her mother to be proud of her, to acknowledge to her friends that Rachel was doing good for the family in the same way that Emily was, but Rachel wasn't sure that would ever happen.

At least she could use her art to bring in a little money. It wasn't a lot, but it had begun to grow steadily over the last year or so, which Rachel was glad for. It gave her a sense of purpose, something she'd been missing since their father had died. But even now, it still didn't feel like it matched up to what Emily was doing.

The worst part was that Emily had managed to find a beau in the midst of all the trouble over the quilt. She'd found Aaron, and his sister, Susan, who was helping her mend the quilt. Emily was pretty sure that Emily would be engaged soon. She'd never seen her sister look at another Amish man the way Emily looked at Aaron. There was an obvious love between them, which, unfortunately, was just another cause of envy on Rachel's part. She didn't have anyone. Wasn't likely to meet anyone either, since she spent so much time on her own, hidden away. Shaking her head to herself, Rachel wondered who on earth would want to spend time with someone like her, someone who was clearly so wrapped up in their own misery that they had nothing kind to say. She wasn't exactly the kind of Amish girl any man would be looking for.

Throwing her pencil down, Emily got to her feet and wandered to the window, looking out across the line of houses and the fields behind them. Sometimes she felt so trapped here, a prison of her own making. She wasn't able to draw when she felt like this, even though commissions were waiting. The weight of responsibility was dragging her down, and Rachel suddenly had a desperate urge to be free.

An Amish Quilt for Christmas

Almost running from her room, Emily rushed through the living room, muttering something about going out for a walk to her astonished mother, before throwing open the front door and walking out. She almost bumped into Aaron and Emily, who greeted her but she simply sidestepped them and walked away. Rachel didn't want to speak to either of them, not now. It was still too much. Still too raw.

Walking blindly, Rachel hardly felt the rain begin to fall on her head, the wind brushing her cheeks with its cool hand. The water pressed into her simple tunic, but she walked on heedlessly. Before she knew it, she was almost soaked through.

Looking around her, Rachel realized with shock that she was quite far from home, and standing in the middle of a field somewhere. Her clothes were almost soaked through and her feet were freezing. By the time she got back home, she'd look like a drowned rat and, truth be told, she didn't want to go anywhere near home if Emily and Aaron were still there.

Paige Millikin

The only other building in sight was a large barn, which looked to be deserted. No-one else was about and so Rachel made her way towards it, the rain now running in rivulets down her cheeks. Walking into the open door, Rachel felt the warmth of the cozy barn begin to pierce through her damp clothes almost at once, and, wiping her face with the back of her hands, leaned against the wall and let out a long breath.

It was only then she realized that she was crying.

An Amish Quilt for Christmas

Paige Millikin

CHAPTER TWO

"Are you all right?"

Letting out an involuntary shriek, Rachel's hand covered her mouth as a man stepped forward out of the gloom, looking quite repentant.

"Sorry," he said, holding up his hands. "I didn't mean to scare you. I thought you'd seen me when you came in."

Wiping her face and again and blinking back the rest of her tears, Rachel drew in a shaky breath.

"I'm sorry to intrude," she said, barely able to meet his gaze. "It was raining and I – "

"You're not intruding," he replied, warmly. "It looks like a bad kind of storm out there. Whatever were you doing walking outside in it?"

Rachel studied him, her breathing slowly returning to normal. He was tall and well built, with a gentle smile and warm brown eyes. "I just needed some fresh air. Going back home would have meant I'd have just been wet through. I thought I'd stop in here for a few minutes. I'm sorry if I'm trespassing, I didn't think anyone was here."

He grinned. "This is my barn, so you don't need to worry about trespassing. You're more than welcome to stop in here until the rain stops."

She managed to smile back at him. "Thank you, uh…" Realizing she didn't know his name, she looked up at him enquiringly.

"James."

"Thank you, James," she finished, moving towards an old rickety chair and carefully sitting down. "I'm Rachel."

"It's nice to meet you," he replied, sitting down on the straw covered floor. "Are you sure you're okay?"

Wondering if he'd realized she'd been crying, Rachel nodded. "I'm fine, thank you. Hopefully, I'll dry off soon." Wanting to change the subject, Rachel looked around at the small barn. "Did you say this was your barn?"

"It is," he replied, waving a hand. "I breed horses and then sell them on. The five down the bottom are my younger ones, and I have another five in the other barn across the field."

"Oh." Rachel let her gaze travel down towards the horses at the other end of the barn, realizing that she hadn't even noticed they were there until he'd pointed them out. How had she managed to miss that? "They're beautiful."

His grin made her heart lurch. "Thanks. They bring me a lot of happiness. It's not everyone who can say that they love what they do, so I feel really blessed."

"That's good," Rachel murmured, not sure what else to say. It was something of a strange situation to find herself in, sitting here with an Amish stranger and chatting quite casually.

"And where do you live?"

Quickly describing her home and family, Rachel made sure not to go into too much detail about them, but saw the questions on his face regardless. Given that she hadn't mentioned her father, that wasn't unexpected, but the truth was

An Amish Quilt for Christmas

Rachel didn't want to talk about him – or was it that she just wasn't used to talking about the past?

"So, I paint a lot," she continued, quickly, hoping he'd forget his questions. "It's the only thing I do really. It brings in a bit of money, I guess."

He looked surprised, and Rachel winced inwardly. Was she really that much of an oddity?

"I've never met an artist before," he said, after a moment. "That's wonderful. You must have been blessed with an amazing skill to be able to help your family with your income."

Her cheeks warmed, and Rachel felt her anxiety disappear. "Thank you," she mumbled, not quite sure how to deal with the compliment. "I mean, it's nothing like what my sister does."

"Oh?"

She shrugged. "Emily teaches at the local school and my brother – he's younger than me – has just got an apprenticeship."

25

There was a brief pause, and Rachel saw the way James frowned, looking a little confused.

"I don't think being an artist makes you any less worthy than a teacher or an apprentice," he said, slowly. "God blesses us each with different gifts and we have to use them wisely."

Rachel stared at him, hardly able to believe what he'd said. That wasn't what she'd expected. On hearing that she was an artist, most other Amish folk smiled politely and asked a few brief questions, but were always much more interested to hear what Emily had been teaching in her class, or how Luke's work was going. It was as though these more traditional roles brought more approval, more acceptance, from those around her. At times, Rachel felt as though the artistic gifts she had made her stick out from the rest, as though she were not fulfilling a need but a want which was frowned upon. Apparently, James didn't think that way. In that one moment, the world around her seemed to brighten, the clouds lifting from her mind for a brief instant.

James smiled at her again, evidently realizing that she was a little lost for words.

"Would you like to come and meet my horses?" he asked, walking towards the back of the barn. "They're all very friendly."

Glancing outside, through the open door, Rachel realized that it was now raining harder than it had previously, it even looked to be a mixture or a heavy rainfall with bits of hail. Shivering slightly, she stepped away from where the cold wind blew in through the open door and walked towards the horses. She smiled as she heard James talking to each one softly, and couldn't help but laugh when one of the horses snuffled at James's shirt, clearly looking for something.

"This one's always cheeky," James grinned, rubbing the horse's velvety nose. "But very loving."

A sudden image flung itself into Rachel's mind. Her fingers began to itch, and she wished she'd had the thought of bringing a sketchbook and pencil out with her on her walk. This was what she wanted to draw. The love between man and beast was both evident and inspiring and sparked her imagination almost immediately.

"I – I was wondering," she stammered, very aware that she barely knew this man at all. "Would it be possible for me to draw the horses sometime?"

"Draw them?" James lifted his eyebrows, but there was a smile tugging at the corners of his mouth. "Would you really want to draw my horses?"

"I think so," Rachel replied, quietly. "There's something about them that just makes me want to get them down on paper." She didn't mention that she wanted to add James into the picture too, although she couldn't help but feel her cheeks flushing a little.

"I'd be honored," he said, softly. "No one's ever wanted to do that before!"

Rachel settled her shoulders and smiled. "Thank you. I might be able to sell a few prints to any of the tourists who come by, so I'll make sure to put the details about your business on the back."

"Just in case any of the *English* are interested in buying a horse," he chuckled, laughter in his eyes.

Rachel couldn't help but laugh too. "Yes, exactly. Maybe we'll be able to get them out of their cars and back onto horses all over again!"

Their laughter echoed around the barn, making a couple of the horses snort and stamp, which only added to their mirth.

"I suppose that means you'll be coming back here, then?" James asked, once their laughter had died away.

Rachel nodded. "Only if that suited you, James. I don't want to interrupt anything or get in your way. I'm happy to paint here alone. I do it most of the time, actually."

He looked surprised. "You paint alone? Without any company? Doesn't that get lonely at times?"

Paige Millikin

It was a probing question and one that Rachel found she didn't want to answer right now. "I wouldn't mind if you were here working if that's what you mean."

Realizing that she wasn't going to open up, he just shrugged and pulled out a treat for the last of the horses. "I'll be around, but you're welcome to come and go as you please. Don't worry about getting in my way. I'll be easily able to work around you."

Her heart lifting, Rachel smiled and stepped towards the door. "It's not raining anymore, so I'd better head on home."

He came towards her, his gaze quite intense. "When do you think you'll be back?" There was a touch of eagerness in his voice that surprised her, making her glance up at him. Their eyes met and something flew between them, something that sent a rush of heat coiling in her belly.

"Tomorrow?" she asked, looking away and stepping outside, her hands rubbing her arms. "In the afternoon?"

"Great," he replied, leaning casually against the door jamb. "I'm looking forward to it."

Turning away, Rachel hurried her steps back towards the main road and then towards her house, feeling much happier and brighter than she had on her way there. She'd found some motivation and met someone kind. *So long as he doesn't ever learn what I've done,* she thought to herself, the quilt coming to her mind and the guilt slowly returning. *He can never know.*

Paige Millikin

CHAPTER THREE

Rachel couldn't help but notice the pained expression on Emily's face as she rubbed her thumb absently. It was more than obvious that Emily was putting in a lot of work to try and get the quilt fixed in time for Christmas, although, if Rachel remembered rightly, her sister had never been much good with a needle. Emily looked directly at her for a moment, and Rachel held her sister's gaze, aware of just how much of a chasm was between them. Pain sliced through her as her sister's wounded expression intensified, her gaze drifting away from Rachel.

Paige Millikin

Rachel lifted her chin and ignored Emily altogether, ignoring the pain in her own heart. "I'm going out," she said, walking over to their mother who was busy making a fresh loaf of bread. "I've finished all of my chores, although I can help you before I go if you have need of me?"

Her mother shook her head and smiled. "I'm quite happy, thank you, Rachel. Emily will be heading back out to school in about an hour and I've got the rest of the afternoon to finish up our laundry and get dinner ready. Don't worry."

Managing to smile back, Rachel tried not think about just how different she was from Emily, pressing her mother's hand for a moment. "I'll only be a few hours."

"Where are you going?"

There was no hint of censure in her mother's voice, just an interest in what Rachel was planning. Normally Rachel gave very little away about what she was doing, but, for whatever reason, she wanted to tell her mother about the new place she'd found.

"I'm going to paint some horses," she replied, leaning against the kitchen counter and letting her mind drift back towards James and his horses. "I stumbled across this barn quite by accident and I've been given permission to paint the horses housed inside."

"By the owner?"

Rachel gave her mother a half-smile, seeing the sudden interest spark in her mother's eyes. "Yes, there is a young man who owns the horses, and he has said I'm more than welcome to paint them."

Her mother frowned. "Is he going to be there?"

Shrugging, Rachel pushed herself away from the counter. "He'll be working, mama, don't worry. I know what's expected of me."

To her surprise, her mother stopped kneading the bread, bent over and kissed her daughter on the cheek. "I know, Rachel. I wasn't intending to give the impression that I was questioning your sense of propriety. I hope you have fun!"

Rachel found that she couldn't answer for a moment, touched by her mother's gesture. "I feel like it's given me the inspiration I've lost, mama," she said, quietly, picking up her things again and walking towards the door. "I'll be back in time for dinner."

"I'd love to see your finished pieces," her mother called, as Rachel left the house. "You know I always love your work."

Rachel mumbled something under her breath and closed the front door behind her, walking down the few steps towards the path. The weight of her art materials seemed to weigh heavier in her hands as the arduous burden of guilt settled on her shoulders once more. Her mother certainly wouldn't want to show any interest in Rachel's work once she discovered what Rachel had done to the quilt.

An Amish Quilt for Christmas

Trudging towards the barn, Rachel tried to keep her thoughts center on the horses, but found herself drifting back towards the way Emily had looked at her. It had come as something of a surprise to realize that Emily hadn't spoken to their mother about what Rachel had done – although whether that was for Rachel's benefit, she wasn't sure. It was going to cause her mother a great deal of pain to see the quilt as it was now, instead of how it had once been, and Rachel knew that pain would only intensify if she discovered that the person behind it had been her own daughter.

Heat hit her cheeks as shame filled her. At the time, Rachel hadn't stopped to think about the consequences of what she was about to do, pushed on by the anger and frustration she felt rolling in her own heart. It wasn't until afterward, when Emily had come back into the house with a face that was pale and drawn that Rachel had truly realized what it was she'd done. At the time, she'd thought that she was just hurting Emily, but the truth was, her mother was the one who was going to hurt the most. Rachel hated that. That hadn't been her intention. She'd just wanted the quilt destroyed, with no knowledge of where it had gone or what had happened to it – with the blame placed squarely on Emily's shoulders. Emily, the sister everyone thought so well of, the one who seemed more responsible and more mature than Rachel could ever be, that had been who Rachel had wanted to hurt. It was only afterward, when it was too late, that she'd realized the true consequences of what she'd done. But still, she wasn't about to either tell her mother or apologize for it.

Making her way to the barn, Rachel's gaze dropped to her toes. The thought of having to tell her mother what she'd done to the quilt made her feel physically sick, so she pushed that idea right to the back of her mind, deciding that she'd never tell her mother the truth. It would be too much to bear. Emily was beginning to fix the quilt and that was probably a good thing. At least it wasn't completely destroyed. Her cheeks burned as she thought of what her mother would have said had she discovered that the quilt was gone, lost forever. Surely now, with Emily and Susan trying to fix it, there wouldn't be too much of an issue? It would be something her mother would be able to deal with, something she'd be able to work through. Trying to tell herself that there was no reason for her to ever tell anyone about what she'd done, Rachel drew in a deep breath and stepped into the barn, leaving all thoughts of her mother, of Emily and of the quilt at the door.

The barn was quiet, with no one else around. Only two horses were in their stalls, the others evidently out to pasture. Rachel took in a deep breath, settling both her shoulders and her spirit. Now she could lose herself in her work, finally able to find a little bit of peace away from her tumultuous thoughts that seemed to surround her whenever she was at home.

"Hey there," she murmured, reaching towards one of the dark chestnut mares. Rachel couldn't help but smile as the horse snuffled her hand, before letting her stroke her velvety nose. A deep sigh left her lips as she just enjoyed being with the animals, seeing the brightness of their eyes and feeling the heat of their breath on her hands.

"They seem to like you."

Rachel jumped but managed not to squeal this time, turning around to see James walking into the barn with a broad smile on his face.

"Hi," she said, feeling more than a little self-conscious. "I only just arrived."

"I know," he replied, with a grin. "I saw you coming."

Wondering whether or not he'd been watching for her, Rachel simply smiled and turned back to the horses.

"Are you planning to paint today?"

An Amish Quilt for Christmas

"Sketch, probably," Rachel murmured, still concentrating on the horses. "I've still got to bring my easel down here and it's pretty bulky."

"I'll help you if you like," James offered, leaning against the barn door. "It wouldn't be too much trouble at all."

A flurry of excitement burst in her stomach, sending sparks shooting through her veins, even though it was an entirely innocuous offer of help. Was it just because she found him easy to talk to? It was as though they'd been friends for a long time, even though it was only the second time they'd met.

"Maybe in a few days' time?" she said, eventually. "I want to get a good few sketches done first."

He nodded. "Sounds good. Just let me know and I'll bring my buggy around one afternoon to get you and the easel – and whatever else you need." He turned to walk away, needing to get back on with his work. "I'll leave you to it. Stay as long as you want, though. There's no rush to leave and I'm sure I'll be in and out of the barn."

Rachel nodded and watched him leave, before settling herself on a large, square bale of hay. Her pencil poised, she studied the horses for a few moments before, finally, letting her pencil sweep across the page.

An Amish Quilt for Christmas

Paige Millikin

CHAPTER FOUR

Several days had passed before Rachel was ready to start painting, even though she'd spent hours down at the barn. Her mother had never asked her any more information about the man who owned the barn, although she was delighted with every sketch that Rachel showed her.

Rachel had to admit that the pull towards the barn and the horses wasn't just because of her painting. The inspiration she'd felt the moment she'd first stepped into the barn hadn't left her, but there was something about James that drew her back there again and again. He was so easy to talk to, and never pushed her into opening up about herself. The strange thing was that, even though he didn't push, Rachel found herself – for the first time in a very long time – wanting to tell him things about herself. It was inconsistent with the kind of person she thought she was, but slowly, ever so slowly, Rachel discovered that James was drawing her out of the castle she'd built around herself.

They talked about a whole range of things, from the weather to the church, from the delights of Christmas to the loss of Rachel's father. Things that she'd never told anyone else, Rachel found herself telling James. He was sympathetic and compassionate, never prodding her to reveal more but just giving her the space and time she needed to work through things. It was a very strange experience for Rachel, and an almost painful one, but one she realized she needed.

Coming out of her shell and talking to James meant that she had to start being honest with both herself and with him. She didn't want to lie to him, but, at the same time, she didn't want to reveal everything about herself to him. Rachel knew for sure that, if she told him the truth about who she was and what she had done, then he'd push away from her for sure.

Trying to appear nonchalant, Rachel smiled at her mother who was busy writing a list of everything they'd need for dinner for the coming week. "Mama, James is coming to pick me up today." She tried to pretend she didn't see the way her mother's gaze shot straight to her almost immediately, continuing to set out her art materials on the kitchen table. "He's coming to help me carry my easel."

"I see," her mother replied, softly. "Are you ready to start your painting, then?"

Rachel nodded, glad that her mother hadn't said anything else about James

Paige Millikin

"It will be nice to meet him," her mother continued, quietly. "I hope you don't mind if I come out to greet him?"

Emily shook her head. "No, of course not." Deep down, Rachel knew what her mother was suspecting, but didn't want to give any weight to that assumption. As far as Rachel was concerned, there was nothing more than friendship between herself and James, although she had to admit that even having a friend was quite unusual.

"Does this explain why you've been smiling a bit more lately?" her mother asked, surprising Rachel. "I don't mean to pry but I can't tell you how worried I've been about you."

"You've been worried about me?" Rachel asked, confused. "Why?"

Her mother sighed and put down her pencil. "Ever since your father died, you've tried to be so strong and resilient, but that's meant that you've built a huge, heavy shell around yourself that no one can really get to."

Rachel tried not to roll her eyes. "And you wish I was more like Emily, right? That I'd be more open and vulnerable, better able to support the family and look after you." She sighed and dropped her gaze to the table, only to feel her mother catch her wrist.

Forced to look over at her parent, Rachel was astonished to see a look of horror on her mother's face, her green eyes wide. She didn't pass any comment for some moments, making Rachel grow more and more uncomfortable with each passing minute.

"I truly hope that is not what you believe," her mother breathed, eventually. "I am quite shocked to hear you say such a thing, Rachel!"

Now even more confused, Rachel shrugged and pulled her hand away from her mother's grip. "I know Emily does a lot for this family, and how much of a support she is to you. I'm sorry I'm not like her."

Paige Millikin

"*No*, Rachel," her mother replied at once, with such a great amount of fervor that Rachel was quite taken aback. "No, you are not to think that way. I have never once asked you to be like your sister, nor will I ever be."

Rachel was surprised to see tears in her mother's eyes, and, as her mother reached for her hand again, took a seat beside her mother at the table.

"When your father died," her mother continued, the pain and grief still evident in her words. "It left such a hole in our lives and we have each dealt with it in our own ways. I wasn't able to be much of a support to you girls, or to Luke, such was my own misery."

"You tried as best you could," Rachel muttered, wanting to reassure her mother. "I understand that."

Waving a hand, her mother shook her head. "I have made a mistake if I've somehow managed to give the impression that I think less of you in comparison to Emily." Her eyes caught Rachel's, burning with intensity. "That is not the case. I have never thought that. If I am honest, I have spent more time praying and worrying over you because I don't know what to do to help you."

A huge surge of mixing emotions rushed over Rachel at once, finally settling in her stomach as it rolled. Her mother had been praying for her? More than for Emily and Luke? Why?

"I've seen you retreat back into your art," her mother continued, softly, her eyes never leaving Rachel's. "I've seen you hide yourself away, keep your thoughts and feelings to yourself – and I've not known how to get through that. Emily talks to me, and so does Luke, so it's simpler for me to know what they're going through. But with you, I'm completely lost."

To Rachel's horror, a single tear dropped from her mother's eye and landed on her cheek, although she quickly brushed it away. A coldness swept through Rachel, as she suddenly became aware of just how wrong she had been about how her mother saw her.

"I – I thought you wanted me to be more like Emily," she said, her voice strangled with emotion. "But I don't know how to be her."

"I have never wanted that for you," her mother replied, almost vehemently. "Never. You are your own person, Rachel, and the talents and gifts you have are uniquely yours. None of my children outdoes the other! I love you all desperately."

There was a huge lump in Rachel's throat which stopped her from replying. Her mother must have seen the pain on Rachel's face, for the next thing she knew, her mother had reached across and pulled her into a hug.

Her mother's arms were tight yet soft, as she murmured quiet things into Rachel's ear. For a moment, Rachel felt as though she was a child again, a child held tightly by their mother when everything

An Amish Quilt for Christmas

else seemed to be going wrong. How often she'd let her mother hold her! It had always been the place where Rachel's pain had slowly ebbed away, where everything had slowly come to rights, but now the exact opposite was happening. Her pain and distress over what she had done only intensified, the twisted knots she'd been tying around herself suddenly growing tighter. This wasn't what she'd expected to hear from her mother.

"Now," her mother said, briskly, sitting back and wiping her eyes with the back of her hand. "This young man of yours is going to be coming soon, isn't he?" She chuckled and dabbed at her eyes with her apron. "No good meeting him with puffy eyes now, is it?"

Rachel tried to smile but found she couldn't. It was as though she was frozen to her chair, her limbs refusing to move. She'd been so wrong about everything. She'd been jealous and envious over an assumption, believing that her mother found Emily more favorable than herself, whereas now she knew that her mother had been struggling to find a way through to her. Hadn't that been her own doing? Hadn't she built up the walls herself, brick by brick, using envy and jealousy as mortar?

"I'm sure I can hear a buggy," her mother declared, breaking into her thoughts. "Come on, now. You don't want to keep James waiting!"

Even the thought of James did little to bolster Rachel's spirits. What would he think of her, if he found out the truth about who she was? Rachel closed her eyes briefly before pushing herself up from her chair and trying to collect her art things. She was just getting further and further into the mire with every step she took. The problem was, she knew that she couldn't find a way out of it alone.

An Amish Quilt for Christmas

Paige Millikin

CHAPTER FIVE

Rachel barely said a word as James greeted both her and her mother, too overcome with everything she felt. She didn't see the way that James' gaze flickered towards her, his expression growing more and more concerned as he continued to talk with her mother.

"Yes, I'm afraid it is just me," he said, drawing Rachel's attention as she finished putting her art supplies into the buggy. "My parents had me very late in their life."

"That sounds very difficult," Rachel's mother replied, sounding heartbroken for him. "Do you live alone?"

"I do."

"Then, if you're not already engaged, I'd be glad to have you join us for Christmas dinner," came the reply. "We already have some other guests so you wouldn't be the only one. I'm sure Rachel would like for you to join us."

Quite startled by her mother's suggestion, Rachel managed to garble something that sounded like an agreement, wondering why she'd not discovered this about James before. This was a big part of his life and something she hadn't known about him. As they'd got to know each other over the last few days, Rachel hadn't once imagined that she'd miss out on something so big. Or was it because she was too busy talking about herself and her own struggles to truly listen to what he had to say? Had she honestly become so distracted in her own pain

An Amish Quilt for Christmas

and suffering, brought on by her own actions, that she'd forgotten how to care for another person?

Her guilt and shame crashed around her yet again. The urge to run away from both her mother and from James hit her full force, to the point that she had to grasp onto the side of the buggy to stop her legs from doing exactly that. As the conversation continued to flow around her, Rachel felt herself sinking deeper and deeper into the mud that she'd deliberately walked into.

She'd thought that getting rid of the quilt would bring her satisfaction - even happiness. Instead, it had just made her world grow darker, and her own heart to suffer even more. The problem was that she couldn't blame her sister or her family for what she felt since she had been the one to try to destroy the quilt. Her own actions were adding to her burden.

"Christmas dinner would be wonderful, thank you," she heard James say, as she climbed up into the buggy. "I'd be glad to meet the rest of your family."

"My daughter, Emily, has a beau who will be joining us, as well as his sister," her mother replied, as James came to sit next to Rachel. "It will be nice to have a full table!"

Rachel murmured her goodbyes, not seeing the look of concern in her mother's eyes as the buggy pulled away. She sat quietly next to James as they made their way down the road towards the barn, her mind filled with all sorts of questions.

"Is something the matter?"

Starting with surprise, Rachel looked over at James as the buggy pulled up next to the barn, realizing she'd been completely lost in thought.

"No, everything's fine."

"Are you sure?"

She tried to smile and shrugged. "I was just thinking."

An Amish Quilt for Christmas

He didn't smile, his serious gaze lingering on her. "What about?"

Rachel sighed and shook her head. "A few things. My family. Christmas. That sort of thing."

Hopping down from the buggy, James walked around to her side to help her down. Rachel noticed that he was frowning heavily, and, not sure why that would be, felt a swirl of anxiety settle in her stomach.

"If you don't want me to come for Christmas dinner, then you just need to say so," he said, gruffly, helping her down from her seat. "I'd prefer you just told me if that was the case."

"No, no!" Rachel exclaimed at once, grasping James' hand in an effort to get him to believe her. "I didn't mean that at all. I'm glad you're coming."

Heat rushed through her as he dropped his head and looked at her. Rachel didn't let go of his hand, even though she knew she shouldn't really be touching him. The last thing she wanted was for

James to believe that she didn't want him around. That would just add to the mess that she needed to, somehow, sort out.

"I want to make sure you're happy about it," James said, slowly, his eyes searching her face. "Something's bothering you but I'm just not sure what that something is."

Aware that he seemed to know her almost better than her own mother and sister did, Rachel dropped his hand and stepped away. It was an uncomfortable feeling, being able to be read so easily. How he could see into her heart so easily wasn't something she could either understand or simply accept - in fact, Rachel wasn't sure she liked it.

"Do you want to talk about it?"

"No," Rachel retorted, spinning around harshly and glaring at him. "I don't want to talk about things, James."

An Amish Quilt for Christmas

He held up his hands in surprise. "I didn't mean to upset you with my question, Rachel. I was just offering to be there for you if you need someone to talk to."

Her anger ripped away from her immediately, suddenly aware of just how rude and hurtful she had been in the face of his kindness. Burying her face in her hands, Rachel took in a few deep breaths, trying not to cry. This wasn't the kind of person she wanted to be, but slowly, so slowly, she was turning into a cruel and thoughtless person.

"I'll take your things inside and then I'd better see to the horses," James murmured, walking past her.

Rachel didn't lift her face from her hands. "Thank you," she whispered, brokenly. She'd pushed him away and, right when she could do with a comforting hand around her, he'd just walked on by. Not that she could blame him. This was entirely her own doing. She couldn't expect him to be there for her when she'd just told him that she didn't need his help.

By the time she'd composed herself enough to walk into the barn, James was already gone. Her art things were settled in a corner of the barn on top of one of the hay bales, ready for her to set up. Rachel tried to feel positive about where she was, about what she was about to accomplish, but all she could think about was her mother, Emily, the quilt, and James. It was all such a mess.

Setting up her easel and her paints, Rachel refused to let a single drop of moisture fall from her eyes, determined that she was just going to carry on as she had done before. The quilt would be shown to their mother over Christmas and, while there would be a bit of a shock, her mother would get over it eventually. Rachel didn't need to say anything about it. James was coming for Christmas dinner, and Rachel had to admit that she was looking forward to spending more time in his company, even if she'd managed to upset their growing relationship already!

An Amish Quilt for Christmas

She'd just have to start focusing a little bit more on him and less on herself, realizing that she'd been so busy concentrating on herself and how she felt that she didn't know that much about him at all.

Time to stop being so selfish and wrapped up in your own world, she told herself, wiping her eyes with the back of her hand.

What she didn't see was that James had been standing at the edge of the barn door, his eyes on her. His mouth twisted in confusion and frustration as he watched her begin to sketch her painting, his eyes filled with worry as he gave her one last look before walking away.

Paige Millikin

CHAPTER SIX

"Rachel, we need to talk."

Glancing up in surprise, Rachel was astonished to see her sister looking down at her, her arms folded and eyes flashing. "What about?"

"Don't feign ignorance," Emily retorted, sounding angry. "You know exactly what it is we need to talk about." She glanced behind her towards the door that led to their bedrooms, worried that their mother might come back down from her room. Their mother always went to bed early but that didn't mean she wouldn't come back to the kitchen for a 'warm glass of milk' like she sometimes did.

"I don't want to talk," Rachel muttered, putting her pencil down and looking away.

"I think we have to," Emily replied, not moving an inch. "What you did has serious consequences."

A stone settled in Rachel's stomach. "Yes, I know."

The bluster seemed to leave Emily at once. She had been standing in a somewhat defensive position, only to now loosen a little, the anger in her eyes fading. "Oh."

"I wasn't thinking," Rachel said, despite herself. "Do you think you're going to be able to fix it?" A sudden desperation filled her as the vision of her mother seeing the burnt and damaged quilt filled her mind.

Emily sat down, her eyes on her sister. "I didn't think you'd be worried about that."

68

An Amish Quilt for Christmas

Rachel felt the urge to explain rise up in her chest, but, having never really talked openly with her sister, didn't quite know what to say.

"Why did you do it?" Emily asked, softly, leaning forward in her chair. "What's happened to you, Rachel?"

"Nothing's happened to me," Rachel retorted, suddenly angry. "I lost my father, that's all."

The look of pain that flashed across Emily's face made Rachel's anger die away almost at once.

"Sorry," she muttered, after a moment. "There's a lot going on right now."

"But you never tell anyone," Emily countered, shaking her head. "I wish you'd talk to me like you once did. We used to be quite close."

"That was before Papa died," Rachel said, sitting back in her chair. "Things can't be the same after a thing like that."

Emily didn't reply, simply watched her sister quietly. Rachel could tell what she wanted to say, although she appreciated that she didn't say anything. Emily wanted to tell her that things could still be the same if she just put in the effort if she was at least *willing* to talk to her family, but Rachel found the very idea too awkward to consider.

"I don't want mama to be too upset," she continued, quietly. "I didn't think about what she would go through once she discovered the quilt was gone."

Emily's expression tightened for a moment, her fingers clasping together tightly. "You wanted it burned completely?"

"I wanted it destroyed," Rachel replied with a touch of vehemence. "I didn't see why you should have something that precious."

There was a long pause. Rachel found that she couldn't look her sister in the eye, suddenly desperate to get away from this situation. Her thoughts turned to

An Amish Quilt for Christmas

James and to the barn, wondering if it was too late to go down there to paint in solitude.

"It wasn't meant to hurt you," Emily replied, eventually. "It's just that I'm the eldest, and, by rights, it comes to me. It doesn't mean that mama loves you any less, or thinks worse of you. Tell me that you don't really think that!"

Rachel found that she couldn't answer. The truth was, she had believed that, for a very long time. It had only been in the last couple of days that she'd begun to question what she'd believed. Her mother had surprised her with the things she'd said, and now Emily was following suit.

"Oh, Rachel," Emily sighed, her eyes filling with tears. "Don't ever think that."

"Why are you so upset?" Rachel asked, gruffly. "Is it about the quilt?"

"I'm upset for *you*," Emily exclaimed, reaching forward and grasping Rachel's hand. "Don't you see that? The quilt is going to be fixed, but the hurt in your heart can't be so easily mended. I want you to know that I'm sorry if I've ever added to your misery by making myself out to be better than you. That's never been my intention."

"I know that," Rachel replied, miserably, more ashamed of herself than ever. She wanted to apologize, to say that she was deeply sorry for what she'd done, but the words just wouldn't come.

"I'm not going to tell mama the truth about what happened," Emily said, getting to her feet. "I wanted to tell you that."

So, if Rachel was going to say anything to her mother about what had happened, it would have to be of her own volition. Emily wasn't pushing her into a corner, demanding that she do it. It was to be her own choice.

"Anyway," Emily continued, with a half-smile on her face. "I'm glad we tried to talk, at least. I know there are a lot of things to work through, for both of us, but I want you to know that I'm here for you if you ever want to talk."

"You're not holding a grudge then?" Rachel asked, surprised at her sister's quick forgiveness.

"Oh, I want to hold a grudge, believe me!" Emily replied, with a small laugh. "I've been spending time talking to Susan and Aaron, and they've been helping me work through things."

"Oh." Rachel's envy surfaced once more, with a great deal of force.

"Mama told me you met someone called James?" Emily asked, evidently unaware of Rachel's upset. "I'm looking forward to meeting him."

"Christmas is only two days away," Rachel realized with astonishment. "He's coming for dinner." She could hardly believe their dinner was drawing closer, feeling sick at the thought of her mother seeing the quilt for the first time.

Paige Millikin

Emily didn't say anything more on the subject, just wishing Rachel goodnight before walking out of the kitchen towards the bedrooms. Rachel was left alone in the kitchen, knowing that Luke, her brother, was out with his friends and wouldn't be back until later. She suddenly felt terribly lonely, and the only face she could think of was James.

He doesn't know the real you, the quiet voice inside said. *You haven't told him about what you did. About how jealous you've been.*

Putting her head in her hands, Rachel began to cry, the pain in her heart growing too much to bear. Telling James what she had done would mean that she'd have to confess to her mother too. Everyone would know what she'd done and there was every chance that James might turn his back on her.

"What am I meant to do?" she prayed, her heart opening up to God for the first time in weeks. "I did something terrible and now I don't know what to do. I wish I'd never done it."

74

An Amish Quilt for Christmas

There wasn't any answer. There was no whisper of reassurance in her heart or a gentle peace settling over her soul. It was as though God was holding Himself back from her, waiting for her to make her choice.

Throwing her shawl over her shoulders, Rachel got up and walked to the window, looking out at the dark sky. She shivered involuntarily, knowing just how cold it was becoming outside. That was very much like her heart. Cold towards everyone who loved her, thinking that they cared about each other more than her. The truth was, she'd pushed everyone away and then blamed them for not managing to pull her out of her shell. It had never been their fault. It had been all her own doing.

What would life have been like if she'd just opened up to them from the very start? If she'd told her mother the grief and pain she'd been struggling with? Maybe she'd never have felt the overwhelming envy and jealousy that had pushed her into burning the quilt. Pressing her forehead against the cool glass of the window, Rachel drew in one long breath, her eyes closing. She was all tangled up inside, her life a mess of knots and struggles, but Rachel knew that she had to be the one to sort it all out. She had to make her way through the quagmire and come out the other side, freed from the mud that clung to her. It was going to be painful, horribly so, but Rachel finally admitted to herself that she had to do it.

What would James think of her? Would he turn away from her, not wanting to pursue their friendship any longer? Rachel sighed heavily, turning away from the window. She had to confess that she was beginning to care for James in a way she'd never experienced before and had hopes that he might, one day soon, ask to court her. If she told him the truth, then that might never happen. She'd end up alienating the one person she wanted to draw near.

"He has to know the truth about who I am," Rachel murmured, making her way to her bedroom. "And then, I have to tell mama."

An Amish Quilt for Christmas

Changing quickly into her night clothes, Rachel was surprised to feel a small amount of peace settle in her heart. Was it because, finally, she was willing to confess what she'd done and ask for forgiveness, no matter what the consequences were?

Thinking that she probably wouldn't get much sleep, Rachel climbed into bed and pulled the covers up to her chin. This wasn't going to be easy, but she was determined to see it through. She just hoped her mother could forgive her.

Paige Millikin

CHAPTER SEVEN

The following morning, Rachel was up at the crack of dawn, racing through everything she had to do to help her mother around the house. Something huge was driving her to get down to the barn to see James, even though she knew it was going to be a difficult conversation. Then, once her mother was finished for the day, Rachel was going to talk to her and tell her everything. It had to be done before Christmas day.

"You're busy this morning," her mother commented with a smile, as Rachel pulled on her boots. "Are you planning to finish your painting? I'd love to see it."

"It's almost finished, mama," Rachel smiled. "And I've managed to complete the commissions I had too, so they're going to be paid for by the end of today."

"You do so well," her mother replied, quietly. "I'm very proud of you, Rachel."

Rachel wanted to tell her, right then and there, that she wouldn't be proud if she knew the truth about what Rachel had done, but she found that the words stuck in her throat.

"There's nothing else you need to help me with here," her mother continued, chuckling. "Emily and Luke both have the day off, and a few days after Christmas too, so we're going to be just fine without you. I know how much that painting means to you."

An Amish Quilt for Christmas

Rachel's gave her mother a sharp look, seeing the slight gleam in her eye. "If you're wondering about James, mama, I'm not sure there's going to be anything more than friendship there...if that."

Her mother frowned. "What do you mean by that? You enjoy his company and he's clearly interested in you!"

Rachel shook her head. "He doesn't know me all that well, mama. Once he does, he might not like what he sees."

"Now you listen to me," her mother replied at once, walking over to her and taking Rachel's hand. "Everyone's got their faults. Everyone's got part of themselves that they don't like, things they've done that they regret, sins that they just keep committing no matter what. That doesn't mean that you're not worthy of someone's friendship or affection."

Hanging her head, Rachel found that she couldn't bring her eyes to her mother's. "It sure feels that way, mama. I've not been the best daughter, or the best sister, lately. In fact, I've been pretty terrible."

She felt her mother's hand touch her chin, lifting her face to meet hers. "Everyone works through things in their own way," came her mother's soft voice. "Some folk have the long path, others have a short one. It's not about the length of time it takes you to get there, it's what you do once you've realized you've got something in your life that needs to change."

"I want to be a better daughter and sister," Rachel replied, earnestly. "I – I want to be more open with you all. I'm just not sure how to anymore."

Her mother laughed softly. "Talking helps, Rachel. Right now, what we're doing now – that is what helps. We'll get there." She leaned down and kissed Rachel's cheek, before holding her in a tight embrace. "I love you no matter what."

An Amish Quilt for Christmas

Those words didn't leave Rachel until she was in the barn, continuing with her painting. There was no sign of James, even though all of the horses were still in their stalls. Rachel appreciated the small gas heater in the corner, knowing she'd be pretty cold if not for that. She appreciated James' thoughtfulness.

The urge to finish her painting pushed her to focus entirely on what she was doing. Deep down, she was worried that he might turn around her tell her that she couldn't come back to the barn again, once she told him what she'd done with the quilt. Putting all of her energy into her work, Rachel continued to work for hours, becoming completely lost in her piece.

James, on seeing her so focused, chose to stand at the barn door and watch quietly, grateful that he'd wrapped up warmly. Rachel was busy putting the final touches to her piece, and he didn't want to interrupt.

Sighing happily, Rachel stepped back and tilted her head to look at her piece. It was as though she'd captured a memory, something that she'd never be able to forget now that it was down on canvas. There were the four horses, their bright eyes all focused on one object, one man – James.

With a start, Rachel realized that she'd painted him almost without being aware of it. Initially, it had been intended to just to be a figure but, now that she looked at it, she saw that she had painted James. He was there, looking at his horses with a smile on his face, just like she'd seen him do so many times.

"Are you finished?"

Rachel turned to see James wander in, his cheeks rosy from the cold.

"I hope you weren't waiting outside!" she exclaimed, suddenly horrified at the thought of him being out in the cold.

He grinned and Rachel felt her heart flutter. "I've enjoyed watching you." He walked around to see her work and Rachel had the sudden urge to stop him so that he wouldn't see what she'd painted.

But it was too late. She saw his eyes widen with surprise and felt heat creep up her neck. "I – I didn't mean it to be you," she stammered, aware of just how foolish she sounded. "It just turned out that way."

"I like it," he replied, softly, turning around to face her. "It's really wonderful. You're very talented, Rachel."

Rachel didn't know what to say, her breath catching in her chest as she realized just how close he was to her.

"I was hoping," he continued, softly, "that you might consider coming courting with me? I know we don't know each other all that well yet, but there's something between us that I want to keep building on."

Paige Millikin

"I've been so selfish," Rachel admitted, dropping her gaze. "I didn't even know your parents had passed away until you mentioned it to my mother."

He shrugged. "That's not a big issue, Rachel and I don't agree that you've been selfish. There's a lot of things we're both working through and they're coming out slowly. I see that as a good thing."

Rachel swallowed hard, knowing what she had to say. "I have been selfish. There's so much of me, of my character, that you don't know."

He frowned. "What do you mean?"

The words came tumbling out of her mouth as though desperate to get out. She couldn't stop the flow once she started, knowing she had to get it all out in one go. "I did something terrible to one of my sister's most treasured possessions, all because I was jealous. I'm so ashamed, especially because she knows it was me now but has decided not to tell my mother. It was her quilt, you see – my mother's quilt.

An Amish Quilt for Christmas

A family heirloom. She gave it to Emily and I was so envious, so jealous that she was being given something so special. I thought it was because of who she was to my mother."

"What do you mean?" he asked, slowly, never taking his eyes from her.

"I believed my mother thought Emily was the better daughter," Rachel whispered, her shoulders slumping and tears beginning to trickle down her face. "She and my mother have always been close, but especially so after my father died. Emily's always been the one to support my mother, to get a good job and bring in money for us all. I felt like a failure, retreating back into myself further and further until I didn't know how to get out."

"So, you took the quilt away from Emily?" James asked, touching her hand. "Have you given it back?"

"I threw it on a fire," Rachel replied, through choked sobs. "Emily's trying to fix it but I know I have to tell my mother the truth. I was wrong to do that. My envy and my jealousy were misplaced, and it's taken me such a long time to realize that. I'm not the person you think I am, James."

Her tears were flowing freely now but, to Rachel's surprise, she felt two strong arms draw her into an embrace until her cheek was resting against James' shoulder. Sobs racked her body for a long time, as the pain and tension she'd carried for so long finally left her.

"I have faults too, Rachel," she heard James say in her ear. "Everyone does. I've done things I regret too, things I'm completely ashamed of. Things that I don't want another person to know." He grasped her shoulders and looked into her face, with a slight smile on his own. "I know how much courage that took," he continued, brushing his thumb over her damp cheek. "And that doesn't stop me from wanting to court you. I'm just glad you feel able to be honest with me."

An Amish Quilt for Christmas

Rachel could hardly believe what he was saying, having never expected such a reaction. She looked into his eyes and saw him smile, her heart bursting to life inside her.

"So, will you go courting with me?" he asked, softly, letting his fingers trail over her cheek before dropping his hands. The hope in his eyes made her smile, and Rachel nodded.

"I'd love that."

Paige Millikin

CHAPTER EIGHT

Luke had gone out with some friends again that evening, even though it was Christmas Eve, which left Rachel, Emily and their mother alone. Rachel was sitting in her chair, her fingers twining over and over again as she thought of what she was going to have to say. She wanted to say it, wanted to get it over with – the problem was that she just didn't know how to start.

"Emily?" her mother asked, interrupting Rachel's thoughts. "How is your quilt going? Will it be ready for tomorrow? I'm looking forward to hanging it up on the wall."

Rachel colored as Emily shot her a quick glance, before smiling at their mother. "It's going to look different than before but yes, it's ready."

Their mother smiled delightedly, looking as though she was about to ask more questions, and Rachel knew she had been given the opportunity she had been waiting for.

"I have something to talk to you about, mama," she began, haltingly. "It's about the quilt."

She felt Emily's eyes on her at once but didn't turn away from what she was about to do. The nausea in her stomach didn't stop but grew in intensity as she looked at her mother, seeing the confusion in her eyes.

"What is it?"

Rachel drew in a deep breath. "I saw you give the quilt to Emily and I was jealous."

An Amish Quilt for Christmas

"Jealous?" her mother repeated. "Oh, my dear! I didn't mean anything by it. It's simply tradition."

"I know that now," Rachel replied, quietly. "But at the time, I didn't. I was consumed with jealousy and so, when Emily hung it outside to air, I did something unpardonable." Each word was becoming harder and harder to say, sticking in her throat until she was forced to stop to get a drink of water. Her mother's face was now slightly pale as she looked from one daughter to the next.

Closing her eyes, Rachel tried to force herself to say the words that would let her mother know exactly what had happened. "I – I put it on a bonfire," she whispered, hating that she couldn't get her words louder than that. "I'm so sorry." Opening her eyes, she saw her mother staring at her in horror, her eyes wide.

"It's not destroyed, mama," Emily said, quickly, trying to draw her mother's attention. "Susan and I have been working very hard to restore it. I'm sure it looks almost identical."

"Why would you do such a thing?"

Her mother's tortured whisper sliced through Rachel's soul. She couldn't look at her mother any longer, dropping her head. "I was jealous," she whispered. "I thought she was getting it because of how much more you appreciated her." She shook her head, tears dripping onto her cheeks. "I know how childish that sounds, and looking back, I can't believe that I did it. I'm truly sorry, mama. I don't know if you will ever be able to forgive me."

There was a prolonged silence, one where Rachel felt every second add to the weight of guilt landing squarely on her shoulders. Her vision blurred as more tears fell, still filled with the horror of what she had done.

To her very great surprise, she saw someone come to stand in front of her, dropping to their knees so that they could look into her face. Rachel, realizing it was her mother, turned her face away, completely and utterly ashamed.

"Rachel," her mother said, softly. "Rachel, look at me."

"I can't," Rachel replied, her voice breaking as she continued to keep her face turned away. "I'm too ashamed."

"Rachel," her mother said again, taking her hands. "I need you to look at me. Please."

Rachel blinked furiously against yet another threatening wave of tears, slowly turning her head back to face her mother, dreading what she would see. However, instead of the anger and upset she'd expected to see, there was only a serenity there. Her mother was, in fact, smiling softly at her, her expression one of forgiveness and love.

"It's only a quilt, Rachel," her mother whispered, softly. "That's all it is. A quilt."

Shaking her head, Rachel sniffed hard. "No, it's not just a quilt. It's a family heirloom. It means so much to you, doesn't it? And I'm the one who ruined it."

"You didn't ruin it," Emily replied, firmly. "I promise you that's the truth, Rachel. Susan has worked wonders with it and I've even managed to add my own little bit."

"I can see just how much you've been hurting," her mother continued, squeezing Rachel's hand. "And that's not what I've wanted for you. You don't know how long I've been waiting for you to open up and tell me what's been troubling you. You've always seemed so strong, coping with the death of your father and all that came with it without needing any of us."

"But I did need you," Rachel burst out, fresh tears falling. "I just didn't know how to open up. I thought that Emily was the one you needed, the one who was helping keep everyone together and so I retreated into my own world." She finally looked into her mother's face, regret swelling inside. "I wish I'd opened up to you sooner. Then maybe none of this would have happened."

Her mother smiled and brushed away Rachel's tears. "You, Emily and Luke are all equally loved, Rachel. You are more important than anything else in this world. I am so proud of all you have achieved."

"I'm sorry I can't do more," Rachel replied, her voice still hoarse. "I know I can't teach like Emily, or build like Luke does."

"That doesn't matter!" her mother exclaimed, interrupting her. "You have different gifts because God has made each of us unique! I love your gifts, and I value you because of who you are. Your contribution to this family is more than I had ever expected and I am so proud of what you do to help. Your paintings bring happiness to others, not just to our own family."

Emily put her arm around Rachel, holding her tightly. "Do you know that I've always wished I could draw like you?" she said, softly, making Rachel stare at her in astonishment. "Plenty Amish girls can teach the children like I do, but I don't think I know another person who can draw like you. In fact, in this community, I know that there's no one else like you, no one else who sells their artwork and keeps on getting commissions. You're truly blessed, Rachel."

Rachel stared at her sister, the pain in her heart slowly beginning to lessen, the deep wounds beginning to heal. "I thought you would hate me because of what I did," she said, eventually, looking from Emily to her mother and back again. "I know how important the quilt is."

"It's nothing compared to the importance of family," her mother replied, leaning forward and embracing Rachel. "These are bonds that can never be broken. I want you to know that I forgive you for what you've done, just as Christ has forgiven me for my own sins."

An Amish Quilt for Christmas

Rachel let her mother hold her for a long time, finding yet more tears escaping as she gave in to what she felt. She had kept everything she thought and felt to herself for such a long time that it was difficult to let her emotions out, but she made every attempt not to hold anything back. It was a healing. A healing that Rachel had needed for a very long time.

"Now," her mother said, briskly, getting to her feet and smiling down at her daughters. "We have lots to prepare for tomorrow's dinner." She lifted one eyebrow and Rachel saw her eyes twinkle. "Is James still coming?"

Just hearing his name brought a blush to her cheeks. "Yes, he said he would." Remembering what he'd asked her, Rachel couldn't help but smile. "I told him everything, so there are no secrets between us."

"That took a lot of courage," her mother replied, quietly. "What was his reaction?"

Paige Millikin

Rachel, feeling the full depth of her mother and sister's forgiveness, shook her head. "He asked me to court him."

"That's wonderful news," her mother replied, gently. "I'll look forward to getting to know him some more."

"As will I," Emily added, as they both got to their feet. "I think this is going to be a wonderful Christmas."

"I think so too," Rachel whispered, a smile on her face and happiness in her heart as she followed her mother and sister into the kitchen.

An Amish Quilt for Christmas

Paige Millikin

Epilogue

The fire crackled as Rachel helped James take off his coat and hang it on the hook by the door. "We got quite some snow last night," he told the gathering as he went by the fire and rubbed his hands together.

"A real white Christmas," Rachel's mother replied carrying another platter of steaming food with a delicious aroma to the dinner table. "You arrived in time for a nice Christmas meal." She sat down at one end of the table with Rachel, James and Luke on one side and Emily, Aaron, and Susan on the other. Her father's chair at the other end of the table was empty. Luke reached across the table and grabbed Susan's hand as everyone else joined hands in prayer before dinner. Though the emptiness of the chair was felt, the room never felt more alive. Rachel's mother glanced at her children's happy faces, the quick long glances from their beau's, and the fellowship of being with one another on this special day. Luke started to talk about his apprenticeship, but kept stealing glances at Susan who was attentively following his story.

After the finished their meal, they gathered around the fireplace. Susan took the quilt out of the wooden crate she brought and unwrapped it. Emily helped her shake the creases out and hang it on the rack on the wall. They all took a step back.

"Oh my!" Rachel's mother exclaimed. Rachel looked over nervously, the guilt manifesting as tears in her eyes. "It's absolutely beautiful."

An Amish Quilt for Christmas

Rachel cleared her throat. James gently reached out and cupped her elbow. She looked up at him and then turned her attention back to the quilt. "Susan, I am so grateful to you. Thank you for helping Emily repair the damage I caused."

"No, it really was my pleasure," Susan interrupted. "I have had the best time getting to know Emily, and now your entire family. Besides, Emily doesn't give herself the credit that she deserves."

All eyes were on the magnificent quilt. The damage was undetectable and Emily started to explain the significance of her row. How each color represented a member of their family intertwined with one another forever. Rachel's heart swelled with gratitude. She looked at the quilt top to bottom. Each row representing a history of their family and room for what was to come.

Paige Millikin

For an excerpt of *Don't Give Up On Me,* a Holiday Romance by Paige Millikin, please read on.

An Amish Quilt for Christmas

Don't give up on me

A Holiday romance

By

Paige Millikin

Copyright © 2016

Paige Millikin

CHAPTER 1.

Beth watched as the sun rose slowly over the sleepy little town of Windings, Colorado. The mountains loomed behind cast in blue and purple hues. As she looked around, Beth took a deep breath and enjoyed the fresh mountain air. Her phone rang, she did not want to answer it though. It was probably Steve, once again locked up in some jail for getting too drunk.

It rang again and this time she answered it. The voice on the line was not who she was expecting. With taunt lips, she breathed out slowly through her nose, so as to not make a sound.

"Ma'am, this is Dr. Whittaker. I am sorry to inform you that your husband Steve is in the hospital. Unfortunately, he was deceased on arrival. We will need you to come in and-"

She barely paid attention as tears rolled down her cheeks. How could this of happened? She knew he had a drinking problem... but she did not imagine it would impair his judgement that much. She hung up without confirming that she would be there. Shock seemed permanently painted on her face. Her eyes darted back up to the mountains that seemed so unaffected by the loss of a human life down below.

Beth took a deep breath in and wiped her face before she headed to the hospital to find out what exactly happened. She only assumed it was alcohol related, he either got into a bar fight or he tried to drive. Either way, she had no idea how she was supposed to handle all... this. He had no one other than her so she was left to follow everything on his partially completed will.

An Amish Quilt for Christmas

Her heart beat slower than normal, it felt as though a million pieces were trying to jam themselves back together only to break apart into more pieces. She sat in the waiting room, waiting for the doctor to come get her. These small hospitals were always so quiet. It left her with time to think.

Time to remember, to feel a deeper loneliness than what had already been settled. She could barely remember the last time she saw him. The real him, not the drunk him stumbling into their Victorian home a few blocks from the center of town, waking her up on a school night as he flopped into the bed and laid there in a silent drunken stupor.

She also had trouble remembering the last meal they ate together. Beth tilted her head to the side as she sighed, tears rolling down her cheek while she tried to remember just a few short years ago he was so happy and easy going. There was always a little sadness in his heart, more so around the holidays but it did not get out of hand until about a year ago. Always working. Always drinking. Choosing to go out and find something else to do while she worked and went to college.

They barely had time for each other… and now they would not have any time for each other. She looked up when the doctor came towards her, asking her to follow. She was not sure she really wanted to, but she stood and followed back to where his body lay. Naked save for a thin sheet and left on a cold slab in the morgue.

"His blood alcohol levels were three times over the legal limit. He slammed into a wall. He went through the windshield and was crushed from the impact. I am very sorry for your loss."

"Uh… thanks," Beth whispered. Seeing him like that made her feel sick. She turned away and rubbed her face with the very tips of her fingers. Flashes of the past caught up to her very quickly in that one moment. Images of him smiling sweetly and sitting across the table from her. Images of him draped half across the table hung over from the night before.

An Amish Quilt for Christmas

Their first date... their last date which was more or less him throwing up in the bathroom while she sat at the kitchen table toying with a wine glass.

"I have class soon... what do you need me to do so I can get there?" Beth said finally, deciding she needed to just go through the motions of the day so she could process this slower.

The doctor looked at her and blinked. "Well... uhm... yes... just one moment and I'll gather the paperwork in a folder for you," he said and walked out. A few moments later he returned. "Here, this has everything you need to fill out. Do you know what his burial wishes are?"

"Yes, he wanted to be cremated and put beside his parents. That's what we'll do then," Beth said. She took the papers and left, she would turn them in later when she got home, but she just could not look at him anymore. She returned home and sat them on the table, grabbing her bag for school and her bag for work. She had to get started. That urge to keep doing what she usually did daily and keep her mind busy pushed her forward and the event to the back of her mind.

Living in a small town like this meant everyone already knew. The shops on either side of the street with their cute little white paned windows were not as inviting today as they usually were. Neither were the soft, but sad, smiling faces from those that had already heard the news.

While she drove her beat up old pick-up truck to the college she glanced at the mountains. They always gave her such a sense of peace, but not today. When she came to the red light at the T in the road where the brick fence on the other side was so obviously destroyed, she began to sob. She wasn't sure how many lights she sat through, but she just couldn't move.

If she had the time she would hide away from everything here, even if just over night. She loved the way the majestic mountains looked, the way they settled in behind the warm little town. Well, it was usually a lot warmer than it was as she sat at the stop light on Main and Junction. Especially at this time of year in late spring. Beth wiped her face and continued on to the college.

The people she passed might have smiled sadly at her, but they did not say anything. Not so soon. She knew they knew, and she knew that they would give her some time to figure out which route of loss she would start on. She tried to hide her look of distress, but it was in her eyes, even as she listened to her instructor lecture and scribbled down notes on her horse diagram.

College had been hard before, always trying to keep up with school and work. Life with Steve had been tough. He had wanted her to spend more time with him. She remembered the first day she had told him she was going back to college. He wasn't exactly pleased, but he did not seem to be completely against it.

"Dr. Bob, the vet that I'm working with, suggested I go back to school today. I think it would be great, I could go back for something that I love doing, especially now..." Beth said, her smile stretched from ear to ear and daydream stars in her eyes. It would not be cheap, but it would be worth it. Or so she thought.

"You're in your thirties, aren't you too old to go back to school?" Steve asked, hung over and practically laid out on the table. His eyes rolled to look at her as he fumbled with a glass of Alka-Seltzer and ginger ale.

"I want to go back and get my degree in veterinary medicine," Beth said softly, her dream *would not* be crushed by him. Not today. "I'm going to go back part time, while I work. I should be able to handle the payments myself so you don't have to worry about anything being turned off or really anything."

"You won't be seeing much of me then, will you?" he said, glancing at the time. "I have to go to work. I won't be home until late. Don't wait up. Do whatever you want. It's not like I can stop you."

An Amish Quilt for Christmas

She had watched him leave with a frown ironed onto her lips, her hands folded in front of her underneath their white wood table. Her eyes just barely seeing the food on her paper plate. Even now as she thought about that day and her decision to talk to Dr. Bob she did not regret that. What she did regret was not talking more to Steve and maybe even getting a little more support from him.

****

Beth parked the truck in front of the veterinarian clinic which was just as quaint as the town it sat in. She looked at herself in the mirror for a minute. She could tell she looked more worn out than normal, her hair was a mess, her eyes had dark circles from fighting back tears. She rubbed her face a little and slapped her cheeks some.

"I'm going to look terrible no matter what I do today…
might as well get this over with anyway. Stay
distracted for now." She chanted to herself then
slowly got out of the truck and was glad she changed
before she left for class. The clinic seemed busy
today from the number of vehicles in the front. She
knew this was the only clinic in town and better than
the ones in surrounding towns. Dr. Bob frequently
made house calls to the farms, but the farmers on the
outskirts brought their smaller animals into the clinic
regularly.

Beth licked her lips and mussed her hair as she
walked into the veterinary clinic where she worked
most days of the week. She gave a very soft smile to
the woman behind the front desk and just walked
back to where Dr. Bob was looking over a patient.
The cute lad wagged his tail seeing Beth walk in.

"Hello, sweetie!" she said softly and waited for a
moment before she got the okay from Bob. She
stepped forward and lightly scratched behind his ears.

"He's doing good today; the worms are completely gone."

"That is good, look at you, you little fighter," she purred and continued to pet him. "I bet your owner will be happy to see you tonight."

"The owner called this morning and said that he isn't coming home until tomorrow so we are boarding Bud here again tonight, but he doesn't have to be completely separate from the other dogs seeing as he's not contagious."

"That is good at least, he seemed so lonely."

"Oh, uh, if this is stepping out of line... Beth, do you need to go home or want to talk about anything?" Bob asked quietly. "You don't have to be here today; you know that right?"

"Of course I know that, if I was that upset I would have called in. I just want to keep busy for now," she said softly.

Bob looked at her, "Well, I am sorry for your loss, if you need to talk about it, then I am here for you."

"Thanks, let's just work, for now, okay?" she asked.

While she was at work she got to be distracted by the animals. She ran her fingers through their fur as she checked them over and took care of them, it seemed to push away all the thoughts of Steve.

Bob watched her closely, wanting to keep an eye on her just in case she started to break down. He was expecting it but did not catch it. He knew there were some problems with Steve. There were few secrets in this town and Steve often closed up the local bar. Still, he wondered why Beth wasn't really seeming to be upset. He thought of her as another daughter and knew she had to be in pain. But Beth always had such a strong work ethic and he knew this may be her way of dealing with such a tragedy.

Beth knew she was being watched by her mentor, a little closer than normal but she did not quite mind actually, it made her feel comfortable that he was willing to make sure she was okay.

She coached herself through the rest of the day, while she cleaned up, while she monitored sick animals... 'Just keep calm... hold it together...' She told herself. She closed her eyes and leaned against the broom for a moment. Her forehead pressed against the handle for just a small moment before she heard footsteps.

"Go home, Beth. Relax, take a bath, drink some wine, if you need someone with you call your friend... Connie I think her name is... Just go, you don't need to be here, it's okay," Bob said and rested his hand on her shoulder.

Beth wanted to fight about it, but she nodded softly, "Okay..." She murmured and gathered her things. She got into the truck, although her house was within walking distance, the college wasn't. She headed home and went straight for her wine glass.

Paige Millikin

'Just one.' She thought to herself and sat on the couch with the TV on. She did not really pay that much attention to it, but she did stare at it. Her mind racing back to Steve, the exciting places he pulled her along to until she wanted to just settle down and try to gain something for herself.

Tears fell down her face as she let herself go. She did not want to call anyone. She did not want to fight with anyone. She did not try to wipe away her tears, they fell freely and soaked her shirt. Her shoulders shook as she just released all the weight of the news, the shock, and everything.

She did not expect to stop crying, but as soon as she did she took a deep breath. She wiped her face and took a shower. Her wine glass wasn't even empty from her first glass. She took note of that and picked it up on her way to the bathroom. Showering slowly after sipping with a bittersweet smile.

"Not as broken up as I thought," she murmured to herself. She was sad, there was that horrible sadness in her heart but it was not as bad as the initial shock. She tilted her head to the side as she washed her hair.

Beth closed her eyes while she let the hot water wash over her. Her stress fell with the water and straight down the drain. She rubbed her face and soon after when to take a nap.

"I'll call Connie in the morning, I'm sure she's busy tonight." She mumbled to herself, glad that she got to be by herself for now. She brushed her hair slowly, thinking about how empty the house felt without Steve's drunken stupor. His awkward rambles filling the place up with how he wanted to move around the world and explore.

She sighed and closed her eyes, almost hearing it. After she took a deep breath she laid down and pulled the blankets up around her. Tired and ready to just sleep for the rest of her life. 'Just let me sleep…' She drifted off slowly thinking.

Paige Millikin

For your copy of Don't Give Up On Me, please visit https://www.amazon.com/dp/B01MZWLHV0.

An Amish Quilt for Christmas

Paige Millikin

ABOUT THE AUTHOR

Paige Millikin

Paige grew up in a small town outside of an Amish community in Ohio. After deciding she had enough winter to last a lifetime, Paige now resides in Florida where she enjoys the sunshine year round. If not in her writing room, you will find Paige running after her two children or trying to find time to have a date night with her husband.

With her own Christian upbringing a major influence in her life, Paige started writing clean, inspirational romances at an early age. She enjoys writing sweet wholesome stories, especially in the Amish and historical genre, that show the beauty of love and how special relationships are meant to be.

Find out more at https://www.amazon.com/-/e/B01MXKAEA3

Paige Millikin

An Amish Quilt for Christmas

If you would like to be notified of new (and free) books by Paige Millikin, you can sign up for a newsletter here.

You can reach Paige at:

mailto:PaigeMillikin@outlook.com

Twitter: https://twitter.com/PaigeMillikin

Facebook: https://www.facebook.com/PaigeMillikin

Paige Millikin

OTHER BOOKS BY PAIGE MILLIKIN

Paige is the author of the Plain & Simple Romance
Series, a short series following a couple who did not
expect to be together.

Plain & Simple: An Amish Romance

Plain & Simple 2: An Amish Courtship

Plain & Simple 3: An Amish Wedding

For a better value, get the set:

Plain & Simple: The Complete Collection

Becoming Amish is an Amish romance where Beth, a
woman living on the outskirts of an Amish community,
suffers a tragedy and is taken in by an Amish family.
Will the way of the Amish pull her into the community
or will the temptations of her English life be too much
for her to leave?

Paige Millikin

The Amish Disappearances follows Nevada who wants her big journalism break. She goes undercover to an Amish community where women had been disappearing from and finds more than she expects in this quaint town.

Second Chances: Life Outside Amish Country is a short story following a woman who is doubting her decision to leave the community. After a chance encounter with a man on rumspringa, will she follow her heart back to her homestead or stay in the city that had captured her desires?

Mending the Heart is an Amish short story of Miriam and Kyle. After Kyle ends their courtship, he goes missing. Will his best friend Jacob and Miriam uncover the mystery and if so, how will they deal with what they find?

Don't Give Up on Me is a full length sweet romance novel set in a small town in Colorado where a woman is trying to pick up the pieces and decide to trust herself in another relationship. Will the spirit of Christmas thaw her skeptical heart?

Twinkling Lights: An Amish Christmas Romance follows an Amish woman who has always put her family first. When she decides to set out on a late rumspringa to find someone to settle down with, she meets her fair share of drama and Christmas miracles.

The Twelve Letters of Christmas is a shorter Regency Romance set in the 12 days before Christmas. A man with a tragic past that makes him loathe the holidays is given a task per day to help him reclaim the joy of Christmas.

The Lord's Country Estate Party is a Regency Romance set in the country estate of a Lord who falls in love with a guest at his party. However, another Lady has ill will towards the new couple and sets out to destroy them.

Murder Outside Amish Country Jonathan feels the call of *rumspringa*, despite his feelings for Miriam. He goes to the city and stays with a young man who had left the Amish community for good. The longer Jonathan stays, the more he doubts the *English* way of life is for him. But when he gets wrapped up in a murder investigation, he is certain that he belongs with the Amish.

The Amish Chances Collection: In the same community as the Plain & Simple series meet Anna & Eli, soon to be engaged. But Eli has a dark secret, one that could tear their relationship apart. Will Eli's best friend Isaac be able to find out Eli's hiding before it is too late?

Amish Chances Book 1: The Amish Courter

Amish Chances Book 2: The Amish Wife

Amish Chances Book 3: The Amish Marriage

Amish Chances: The Complete Collection

An Amish Quilt for Christmas

Ring of Abduction- Set in the same community as the Plain & Simple series meet Malachi. His brother Aaron is missing and Malachi is certain there is foul play. Sophie is the detective who is working to find Aaron and she believes his disappearance is linked to other crimes that have occurred outside this peaceful community.

The newest series in the Plain & Simple Community is An Amish Midwife. Charity is a midwife from the English world with an Amish past. Follow her journey as she helps the women in the nearby Amish community.

An Amish Midwife Collection

Book 1: An Amish Midwife

Book 2: An Amish Midwife Comes Home

Book 3: An Amish Midwife at Peace

Book 4: An Amish Midwife Blessing

Paige Millikin

An Amish Quilt for Christmas: In this two-part holiday short story a family heirloom goes missing and Emily is determined to find out who took it. After she finds it nearly destroyed, she is devastated. With the death of her father taking great pains on her family, her mission to repair the quilt with the help of Susan and her brother Aaron makes long lasting changes in her life.

An Amish Quilt for Christmas Book 1: Emily

Made in the USA
Middletown, DE
02 April 2018